ADVERTISING

THERMOMETERS

IDENTIFICATION & VALUE GUIDE

Curtis Merritt

COLLECTOR BOOKS

A Division of Schroeder Publishing Co., Inc.

The current values in this book should be used only as a guide. They are not intended to set prices, which vary from one section of the country to another. Auction prices as well as dealer prices vary and are affected by condition as well as demand. Neither the author nor the publisher assumes any responsibility for any losses that might be incurred as a result of consulting this guide.

On the Cover:
Ramon's Brownie Kidneys Laxative, tin, 21½" x 9", 1930s,
$350.00 – 400.00.
Holland Custard Ice Cream, 12" dia., 1960s – 1970s, $200.00.
Suncrest Bottle, 16" x 4", 1960s, $200.00.
Kentucky Tavern, 12", 1950s, $125.00.
Keen Kutter, 12", 1950s, $400.00.
Drink 3V Cola, 12", 1960s, $150.00.
Little Squirt, 9", 1960s, $250.00.
AC Spark Plugs, 12", 1950s, $450.00.
Shell Shellzone Anti-freeze, 5", 1940s, $300.00.
Texaco, plastic, 7" x 3", 1950s, $75.00.
Miss Sunbeam, 12", 1950s, $700.00 – 750.00.

Cover design by Beth Summers
Book design by Karen Smith

Searching for a Publisher?

We are always looking for knowledgeable people considered to be experts within their fields. If you feel that there is a real need for a book on your collectible subject and have a large comprehensive collection, contact Collector Books.

Collector Books
P.O. Box 3009
Paducah, Kentucky 42002-3009

www.collectorbooks.com

Copyright © 2001 by Curtis Merritt

CONTENTS

ACKNOWLEDGMENTS

This being my first book, I had a lot of help from friends and family. Advertising and promotional things have always fascinated me. I am proud of this book because it shows one tool that has been used to advertise for many years — the thermometer.

When I first began collecting, I mainly dealt with old advertising distillery jugs and signs. It wasn't long before I was also interested in advertising thermometers and the colors and graphics used on them. There are so many that you could go a lifetime and not see all of them. They range from oil related to soda. From the turn of the century and before, almost every business has used thermometers to advertise their services or products.

This book is compiled from several large thermometer collections. I would like to give special thanks to these people for their help in producing this book. Mac and Priscilla Costello of Clinton, Indiana; Bill and Mary Jo Edwards of Indianapolis, Indiana; Eddie and Linda Defew of Salem, Kentucky; Keith and Pam Miller of Booneville, Indiana; and Mark Downing of Clinton, Indiana. Thanks also to Amy and Clint Merritt, Nathan Mayfield, Matthew Fitzgerald, and David Coomes.

PREFACE

I decided to put together this price guide one day while talking to a dear friend of mine, Keith Miller. Keith and I have been many a mile together. Keith has a fabulous collection of advertising thermometers that he has acquired over the past 15 years. He said the first thermometer he ever bought was an old rusty Coca-Cola one. It was in an old chest freezer. Someone had used it to determine the temperature in the freezer. I asked Keith which thermometer was his favorite and he said that it was the Miss Sunbeam Bread. Keith said the thing about these advertising thermometers is that they show a lot about the history of our country's products and services. There is no end to where these thermometers may go.

I was soon introduced to a man named Mac Costello. Mac is from Clinton, Indiana. He is a very knowledgeable and avid collector of these thermometers. Over the past 18 – 20 years, Mac says he has collected over 3,500 of them. According to Mac, getting the rare and hard-to-find thermometers is very difficult. You have to pay for what you get. I asked Mac what he thought the future holds for the collectors of these advertising thermometers. He said it is a great investment and that due to the Internet these rare items are easier to find. Mac's favorite thermometer is said to be the Big Drink Orange Kiss. Mac introduced me to his friend Mark Downing who also had an impressive collection. Mark loves the Frosties root beer thermometers.

Bill Edwards was from Indianapolis, Indiana. He had the nicest soda thermometer collection I've seen.

PREFACE

Bill said his favorite is the Little Arch Top Coca-Cola thermometer. Finding a thermometer you had never heard of is the most fascinating thing about collecting to Bill.

In Salem, Kentucky, I met Eddie Defew and his wife Linda. Eddie has been collecting for 15 years. He said collecting these advertising thermometers with the different graphics reminds him of his childhood. I told Eddie I thought there was a wide range of areas to focus on when collecting these thermometers. Eddie agreed and said he thought a person should pick out a type of thermometer he's really interested in and go from there. When I asked Eddie if he had a favorite he said no. He likes them all.

PRICING

The assigned prices in this book are based on retail and auction sales. The thermometers are priced in mint condition. When a thermometer is not in mint condition, the price will drop according to condition and age. There will be that occasional someone who will say they bought a mint thermometer cheap. Although you may get lucky and find something like this, it is not all that common.

Due to increased Internet auctions, these more valuable thermometers have become more accessible. They are not only found at auctions, antique shops, and flea markets but can also be bought and sold from your home computer.

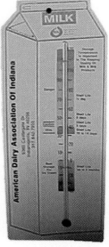

American Dairy Association of Indiana, cardboard, 9½" x 4", 1990s, $5.00 – 10.00.

For Uniformity Better Feed, Super Solubles, 20½" x 9", 1950s, $125.00.

Plant Bo-Jac Hybrid Seed Corn, Wesley A. Scroggin & Sons, cardboard, 6" x 2", $25.00.

Bowman Milling Co., 16½" x 6½", 1950s, $75.00 – 100.00.

Bupp's Dairy,
Hanover, PA,
celluloid,
6" x 2", 1940s,
$65.00 – 85.00.

Case Tractor,
12" dia.,
1960s – 1970s,
$125.00 – 150.00.

Center Brick and
Planters Tobacco
Warehouse,
Owensboro, KY,
13" x 5", 1970s,
$35.00.

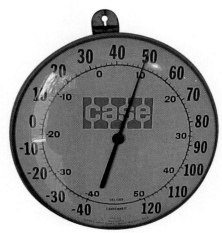

Clinton Center Mill, metal frame with glass front silhouette, 5" x 4", 1950s, $35.00 – 50.00.

Critic Feed, 12" dia., 1960s, $100.00.

AGRICULTURE

Dairymen, Inc.,
tin, 16" x 6",
1980s, $50.00.

DuPont
Agricultural
Products,
10" x 4",
$35.00 – 40.00.

Farm Bureau Co-op, 7" x 2½", 1950, $75.00 – 100.00.

Farmers Co-op Store, Owensboro, Ky., 13" x 4", 1960s, $35.00.

The Farmers Store, Inc., 13" x 4", 1950s, $50.00.

Farm Fans, Inc.,
1970s,
$100.00 – 125.00.

Quaker,
Ful-O-Pep Feeds,
embossed,
25½" x 9½",
1950s,
$275.00 – 300.00.

Gibson County
Farm Bureau
Co-op, 13" x 4",
1960s, $35.00.

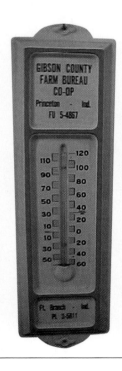

Golden Acres
Hybrid Seeds,
17" x 7", 1970s,
$75.00.

Haines Dairy
Farm, 7" x 4",
1960s, $40.00.

Happy Farmer
Feeds, 12" dia.,
1950s,
$100.00 – 125.00.

AGRICULTURE

Henry Farmers Co-op, 7" x 3", 1940s – 1950s, $65.00.

John Deere, metal, 13" x 13", 1970s, $50.00 – 75.00.

John Deere, #97 Chad Little, Roush Racing Team, plastic, 1990s, $20.00.

Nothing Runs
Like a Deere,
John Deere,
plastic,
9½" x 11",
1990s, $20.00.

K-Millwork,
13" x 3", 1960s,
$50.00.

King Plows Co.,
wood, 5" x 12",
1930s, $150.00 –
200.00.

AGRICULTURE

Klusken
Turkey Farm,
plastic, 7" dia.,
$75.00 – 100.00.

Lone Star Brand
Feed Fertilizer,
12" dia., 1960s,
$150.00 – 175.00.

Lucky Horse
Feed, Earl's Feed
& Grain,
12" dia., 1990,
$20.00 – 25.00.

Francis H. Lueken and Son, Ferdinand, Indiana, 12" dia., 1960s, $100.00.

All Season, McMess Flexible Feed Programs, 12" dia., 1960s, $130.00 – 150.00.

Mercantile, The Poultry Health Engineers Co., 10" dia., 1960s, $250.00 – 300.00.

AGRICULTURE

Migro Seed Corn, 12" dia., 1970s – 1980s, $75.00 – 100.00.

Use Nunn-Better Flour and Mixes, Nunn-Better Feeds, red on white, 10½" x 3½", 1950s, $50.00.

Nunn-Better Flour, Nunn-Better Feeds, black on white, 10½" x 3½", 1950s, $50.00.

Pillsbury's
Best Feeds,
Pam Clock Co.,
12" dia., 1950s,
$400.00 – 450.00.

Compliments of
Your Milk Hauler,
Agee Pritchard
Marshall, Ind.,
8" x 3¾", 1930s,
$75.00 – 100.00.

Super **Rainbow** Premium Plant Food, Pot of Gold Fertilizer Materials, 13" x 4½", late 1960s, $100.00 – 125.00.

Ruxer Tractor Co., Inc., St. Meinrad, Ind., plastic, 7", 1950, $250.00.

Smitty's Farm Equipment Store, Jasper, Ind., Oliver and New Idea, 11" x 4", 1970s, $35.00.

Spencer Equipment Company, Rockport, Ind., 12" dia., 1950s, $350.00.

Stull's Hybrids, 12" dia., $200.00.

AGRICULTURE

Supersweet
Feeds, 12" dia.,
1970s, $100.00.

Taylor Feed and
Produce Co.,
painted mirror,
22" x 12", 1960s,
$100.00.

Geo. P. Wagner
Co., tin, 13" x 4",
1940s, $250.00.

Amprol, It Pays to Feed **Wayne Feeds**, 10" dia., 1950s, $75.00.

Wirthmore Feeds, Serving the Poultry and Livestock Industry, 15" x 8", 1960s, $50.00 – 75.00.

Wisconsin's Finest Dairy Heifers, 11" x 4", 1970s, $50.00.

UTOMOTIVE

American, Greer
and Hamilton
Oil Co., 7" x 3",
1960s, $100.00 –
125.00.

Atlas Perma-
Guard Anti-
freeze, Does Not
Evaporate, 1930,
$300.00 –
350.00.

Bachelder's Ser-
vice Stations,
Athol, Mass., tin,
2" x 2¾", 1940s,
$35.00 – 50.00.

Boyll & Sons
Motor Co., paint
on mirror,
9" x 8", 1940s,
$100.00 – 125.00.

Bunn Bros.,
Belleville, Ill.,
13" x 4", 1958,
$35.00.

Trojan Batteries,
Brach Auto
Supplies,
10½" x 3½",
1960s, $45.00.

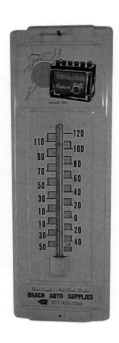

Cāsite Oil,
12" dia., 1950s,
$125.00 – 150.00.

Cāsite Oil,
12" dia., 1950s,
$125.00 – 150.00.

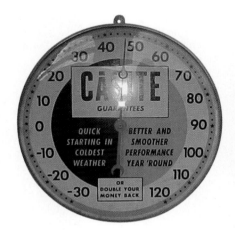

Champion
Dependable
Spark Plugs,
wood, 21" x 5½",
1930s, $200.00.

Chevron, lollipop,
7" x 2½", 1950s,
$50.00 – 75.00.

Corvette,
plastic front,
18½" dia., 1980s,
$65.00 – 85.00.

Craig's Service
Station,
cardboard,
9½" x 6½",
1950s,
$25.00 – 35.00.

Curry Quick Co.,
metal frame
with plastic
front, 6" x 4",
1950s,
$35.00 – 50.00.

Jimmy's Service, 100% Fresh, Delco Batteries, cardboard, 5¾" x 3", 1950s, $40.00 – 50.00.

Dulgar Chevrolet, Inc., 4" x 13", $40.00.

D-X Motor Fuel, Diamond Motor Oil, 9" x 4", 1940s, $100.00.

Gulf, Houk's Service Station, 7" x 2", 1950s, $75.00 – 85.00.

Gulf, No-Nox Gulf Pride Oil, 26" x 7", $200.00 – 250.00.

Gulfpride, The World's Finest Motor Oil, Gulf, 12" dia., 1950s, $250.00.

Gulf, Sam's, plastic with window extenders, 8½" x 3½, $100.00.

Gulf, Sam's, 7" x 2", 1950s, $75.00 – 85.00.

Harley-Davidson Racing, plastic, 3⅓" x 1½", 1992, $15.00.

Hester Batteries, 12" dia., 1960s, $100.00 – 125.00.

Lannert Parts Co., Inc., Automotive Distributors, Evansville, Ind., wood, 14½" x 4", 1940s, $75.00.

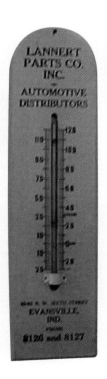

Lifeline Fan Belts, Flexible Radiator Hose, 10" dia., 1960s, $50.00 – 75.00.

Marathon, Petroleum Products, 14" x 4", 1960s, $55.00.

Marathon, Jack Scott, Running Man, 10½" x 4", 1940s, $150.00 – 200.00.

Marathon,
Running Man,
lollipop,
7" x 2½", 1950s,
$250.00 – 300.00,
rare.

Maremont,
Mufflers and
Pipes, diecut,
22½" x 11",
1980s, $65.00.

Mightyplate,
T.B.C.,
Texas Refinery,
23" x 7", 1970s,
$125.00 – 150.00.

Mineweld Company, Everything for the Welder, Call L-6294, Terre Haute, Ind., 16" x 5", $75.00.

Mineweld Company, Everything for the Welder, Call L-6294, Terre Haute, Ind., 16" x 5", $75.00.

AUTOMOTIVE

S & P Auto Parts,
Napa, 13" x 3½",
$50.00.

Peak Antifreeze
& Coolant,
Fred W. Phillips
Distribution,
10" dia., 1980s,
$75.00.

Pennzoil
Motor Oil,
22½" x 5¼",
1940s,
$300.00 – 325.00.

Polarine ISO-VIS Motor Oil, Does Not Thin Out, porcelain, 6'4" x 18", 1930s, $1,200.00 – 1,500.00.

Prestone Anti-freeze, porcelain, 36" x 9", 1940s – 1950s, $150.00.

AUTOMOTIVE

Publix Oil Corp.,
10¾" x 3", 1970s,
$60.00 – 75.00.

Risolene,
The Oil Alloy,
25½" x 10",
1930s,
$350.00 – 400.00.

Sealed Power
Piston Rings,
27" x 8", $125.00.

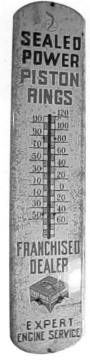

Shell, Elzer Oil
Co., 14" x 4",
1970s, $45.00.

Shell, Elzer Oil
Co., 12" x 3",
1950s, $50.00.

Shell, Elzer Oil
Co., 12" x 3",
1970s, $40.00.

Shell, Furnace Oil, tin, 17" x 3", 1940s, $200.00.

Shell, Shellzone Anti-freeze, 5" dia., 1940s, $300.00.

Sinclair, 7" x 3", 1950s – 1960s, $75.00 – 100.00.

Skelgas, Butler's Skelgas, Inc., lollipop, 7" x 2½", 1950s, $125.00 – 150.00.

Standard, Home Heating Oils, tin, 12" x 3", 1950s, $75.00.

Standard Oil,
14" x 4", 1970s,
$45.00.

Ray Loheider,
Standard Oil, tin,
14" x 4", 1970s,
$40.00.

Standard Oil, Wm. M. Tooley, 14" x 3", 1970s, $45.00.

R.H. Stoltz Co., 8½" x 3", $35.00.

Texaco, Firestone, tin, 10" x 3", $25.00.

Texaco (gas sign), S.A. Randall & Sons, Brazil, Ind., plastic, 1950s, $75.00.

Independent Oil
Co., **Texaco**,
Leitchfield, Ky.,
9" x 4", 1970s,
$50.00.

Texaco, Indepen-
dent Oil Co., 7" x
3", 1950s, $75.00.

Texaco, Motor Oil
Heavy, 16" x 6",
1998, $16.00.

Texaco,
Jay O'Flynn &
Son, 13" x 14",
1970s, $35.00.

Wabash Independent Oil Co.,
Goodyear,
6" x 1½", 1970s,
$35.00 – 50.00.

West End Motors,
Mercury, Canadian, metal with
glass front,
7" x 5", 1950s,
$35.00 – 50.00.

Wester Oil Co., plastic, 6" x 2", 1950s, $75.00 – 85.00.

Willy's Automobiles, Overland, cardboard, 11" x 3", 1950s, $15.00 – 20.00.

Ale-8, 12" dia.,
1970s – 1980s,
$100.00 – 125.00.

A & W,
27" x 9", 1980s,
$150.00 – 200.00.

B-1 Lemon-Lime,
16" x 4½", 1960s,
$100.00.

B-1
Lemon-Lime
Soda,
16½" x 4½",
1950s,
$150.00 – 175.00.

B-1 Lemon-Lime
Soda, 12" dia.,
1950s, $250.00.

Bardenheiers
Fine Wines,
12" dia., 1961,
$125.00 – 175.00.

Barq's, 25" x 7½",
1960, $125.00.

Barq's Root Beer,
gray, 24" x 7½",
1980s, $150.00.

BEVERAGE

Barq's, 26" x 10",
1950s, $150.00.

Barq's, 26" x 10",
1950s, $150.00.

Belfast Old
Fashioned Mug
Root Beer,
12" dia., 1950s,
$275.00 – 325.00.

Big Red, 12" dia., 1950s – 1960s, $175.00 – 200.00.

Big Red, tin, 16" x 6", 1960s, $150.00.

Bireley's Non-Carbonated Beverages, 26" x 10", 1950s, $250.00.

Bireley's,
embossed tin,
14" x 6", 1960s,
$125.00 – 150.00.

Bireley's,
16" x 6", 1959,
$100.00 – 125.00.

Bireley's,
12" dia., 1950s,
$200.00 – 225.00.

Bireley's,
10" x 26", 1950s,
$150.00 – 200.00.

Booster,
9" dia., 1950s,
$75.00 – 100.00.

Brownie
Chocolate,
12" dia.,
1950s – 1960s,
$225.00 – 250.00.

Brownie
Chocolate,
12" dia.,
1950s – 1960s,
$225.00 – 250.00.

Bubble Up,
15½" x 6", 1980s,
$75.00 – 100.00.

Bubble Up, tin,
17" x 5", 1960s,
$100.00.

Bubble Up, tin,
17" x 5", 1960s,
$100.00.

Bubble Up,
15½" x 6",
1970s – 1980s,
$75.00 – 100.00.

BEVERAGE

The Soft Whiskey,
Calvert Extra,
12" dia., 1960s,
$275.00 – 325.00.

Calvert Extra,
12" dia., 1970s,
$125.00 – 150.00.

Canada Dry
Orange,
12" dia., 1961,
$350.00 – 400.00.

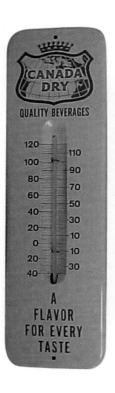

Canada Dry,
14" x 4", 1970s,
$150.00 – 175.00.

Champale,
8" x 16",
1950s – 1960s,
$75.00 – 100.00.

Champale Malt
Liquor, tin,
8" x 8", 1950s,
$50.00 – 75.00.

BEVERAGE

Cheer Up,
masonite
material used
during war years,
16" x 5", 1940s,
$250.00 – 300.00.

Chocolat Royale,
13½" x 6", 1960s,
$150.00.

Chocolate
Soldier,
12" dia., 1950s,
$250.00 – 275.00.

Drink
Lively Limes,
Cloverdale,
12 dia., 1950s,
$175.00 – 225.00.

Cloverdale
Ginger Ale,
Pepsi product,
12" x 12", 1950s,
$225.00 – 250.00.

Cloverdale
Ginger Ale,
12" dia., 1950s,
$250.00 – 275.00.

Coca-Cola,
Coke, You Can't
Beat the Feeling,
porcelain on
stamped metal,
Belgium, 23" x 9",
$200.00 – 300.00.

Coca-Cola, trade-
mark registered,
tin, 17", 1950s,
$200.00.

Coca-Cola,
17", 1960s,
$125.00.

Coca-Cola,
gold bottle, tin,
16" x 7", 1930s,
$300.00 – 350.00.

Drink **Coca-Cola**, 12" dia., 1950s, $200.00.

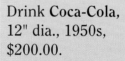

Coca-Cola, brass, 29" x 8", $175.00.

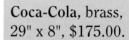

Enjoy **Coca-Cola**, plastic, 17" x 6¾", 1960s, $65.00.

BEVERAGE

Drink **Coca-Cola**,
Thirst Knows No
Season, masonite,
17" x 6¾", 1940s,
$375.00 – 400.00.

Drink **Coca-Cola**,
6½" x 2½", 1970s,
$30.00 – 50.00.

Drink
Coca-Cola,
Delicious and
Refreshing, 1940s,
$325.00 – 350.00.

Coca-Cola,
Trade Mark
Registered,
Bottle Pat'd
Dec. 25, 1923,
15½" x 5",
$300.00.

Drink Coca-Cola
In Bottles, Serve
Coke at Home,
9" x 2½",
1950s – 1960s,
$200.00.

Drink Coca-Cola
in Bottles,
Refresh Yourself,
30" x 8", 1950s,
$400.00 – 425.00.

Coca-Cola,
heavily embossed
brass, considered
to be bootlegged
by some, highly
sought after by
others,
17" x 5¼", 1980s,
$75.00 – 100.00.

Drink Coca-Cola,
"double," tin,
15½" x 7", 1940s,
$350.00 – 375.00.

Drink **Coca-Cola**, arch, 3½" x 2", 1930s – 1940s, $1,800.00 – 2,000.00.

Things Go Better with Coke, Drink **Coca-Cola**, 12" dia., 1960s, $300.00.

Drink
Coca-Cola
in Bottles,
12" dia., 1950s,
$200.00.

Drink **Coca-Cola**
In Bottles,
Quality Refresh-
ment, 9" x 3",
$200.00 – 250.00.

Drink **Coca-Cola**,
5¢, Delicious
Refreshing,
1990s, $20.00.

Coca-Cola,
formed bottle,
tin, 17", 1950s,
$200.00.

Cook's Beer and
Ale, Always Fine,
12" x 4", 1940s,
$200.00.

Cott Ginger Ale,
15" x 7",
1960s – 1970s,
$125.00 – 150.00.

Crystal Club
Beverages,
14" x 6", 1950s,
$125.00 – 150.00.

Dad's Root Beer,
27" x 7½", 1950s,
$150.00.

Dad's Root Beer,
25" x 10",
$200.00 – 220.00.

Dad's, The
Original Draft
Root Beer,
27" x 7½", 1950s,
$150.00 – 200.00.

Diet Dad's
Root Beer,
27" x 7½", 1950s,
$175.00 – 200.00.

Delaware Punch,
plastic frame
with plastic front,
11" dia., 1970s,
$200.00 – 250.00.

Sugar Free
Diet-Rite Cola,
12" dia., 1960s,
$125.00.

Diet-Rite Cola,
12" dia., 1960s,
$125.00.

Diet-Rite Cola,
12" dia., 1960s,
$125.00.

Double Cola, bot-
tle shaped, diecut
tin, 13" x 4",
1938, $450.00 –
500.00.

Double Cola,
17" x 5", $100.00.

Double Cola, white with red lace, 17" x 5", $100.00.

Double Cola, red, 17" x 5", $100.00.

Double Cola, two different thermometers, 17" x 5", 1950s – 1960s, $100.00 each.

Double Cola, blue, 17" x 5", $100.00.

Double Cola, red with white lace, 27" x 8", $100.00 – 125.00.

Double Cola, blue starburst, 27" x 8", 1940s, $100.00 – 125.00.

Double Cola, blue with yellow lines, 17" x 5", $100.00.

Double Cola,
world outlined,
12" dia., 1960s,
$225.00 – 250.00.

Dr. Pepper,
11" dia.,
1950s – 1960s,
$150.00 – 175.00.

Dr. Pepper,
12" dia., 1960s,
$225.00 – 250.00.

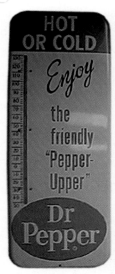

Dr. Pepper,
25" x 10",
1950s, $250.00.

Dr. Pepper,
26" x 7", 1950s,
$150.00 – 200.00.

Dr. Pepper,
27" x 8",
1960s, $125.00.

Dr. Pepper, tin,
16" x 4½", 1950s,
$150.00 – 200.00.

Dr. Pepper,
12" dia., 1960s,
$300.00 – 350.00.

Dr. Pepper,
12" dia., 1950s,
$200.00 – 250.00.

Dr. Pepper,
12" dia., 1950s,
$175.00 – 250.00.

Dr. Pepper,
painted
stamped metal,
25½" x 9¾",
1940s,
$400.00 – 450.00.

Dr. Pepper, tin,
16" x 4½", 1950s,
$150.00 – 200.00.

Dr. Pepper,
27" x 8", 1960s,
$125.00.

Dr. Pepper,
painted diecut,
17" x 5½", 1938,
$600.00 – 650.00.

Dr. Pepper, tin,
12" x 7", 1970s,
$50.00.

BEVERAGE

Dr. Pepper,
16" x 6½",
$400.00.

Dr. Pepper,
17½" x 5",
1940s,
$550.00 – 600.00.

Duke Beer,
22" x 11",
1970s – 1980s,
$35.00 – 45.00.

Esslinger's
Premium Beer,
Little Man Ale,
painted masonite,
16" x 4½",
1940s war years,
$300.00 – 325.00.

Drink 50/50,
12" dia.,
1960s – 1970s,
$200.00 – 225.00.

Fleishmann's Gin-Vodka-Whiskey, tin with 6" glass front, 9" x 9", 1960s, $75.00 – 100.00.

Frank's, Dry Ginger Ale Fruit Beverages, 12" dia., 1950s, $250.00 – 275.00.

Fresca, plastic, 17" x 6¾", 1960s, $75.00.

Frostie Root Beer, 12" dia., 1970s – 1980s, $100.00 – 125.00.

**Frostie Rootbeer,
12" dia., 1980s,
$125.00 – 150.00.**

**Frostie,
diecut plastic,
15" x 12", 1970s,
$125.00 – 150.00.**

Gilbey's Gin,
diecut
metal, 1970,
$75.00 – 100.00.

Gilbey's Gin and
Vodka, 9" dia.,
1960, $100.00.

Grapette Soda,
6" x 3",
1960s–1970s,
$40.00 – 50.00.

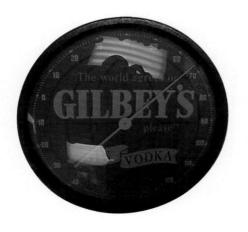

Grapette Soda,
Thirsty or Not,
1950s, $250.00 –
300.00.

Fruit Drinks,
Green Spot,
23" x 7",
$125.00 – 150.00.

Green Spot,
16" x 5", 1950s,
$250.00 – 300.00.

Hires Root Beer, painted diecut metal, 27½" x 8", 1960s, $250.00 – 300.00.

Genuine **Hires Root Beer,** Blue Dot, 27½" x 8", 1970s, $225.00 – 275.00.

Hires Root Beer, 12" dia., 1970s, $125.00 – 150.00.

Hires Root Beer,
12" dia., 1970s,
$125.00 – 150.00.

Hires Root Beer,
tin, 27" x 8",
1940s – 1950s,
$200.00 – 250.00.
Watch for repro-
ductions which
are not as wide.

Hires Root Beer,
painted diecut,
27½" x 8", 1950s,
$300.00 – 350.00.

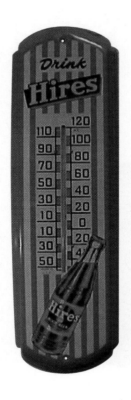

Honee Orange,
16" x 5",
1960s – 1970s,
$150.00 – 200.00.

IBC Root Beer,
26" x 9", 1970s,
$175.00.

Cherry Smash
Icee, 12" dia.,
1967, $225.00.

BEVERAGE

Imperial Whiskey
by Hiram Walker,
12" dia., 1960s,
$75.00 – 100.00.

Jim Beam,
25½" x 9½",
1960s, $125.00 –
150.00.

John Collins,
40" x 10½",
1950s,
$500.00 – 600.00.

Kayo Chocolate,
13½" x 6", 1963,
$100.00 – 125.00.

Orange Kist,
Spanish, 39" x 9",
1960, $275.00.

Orange Kist,
39" x 9", 1960s,
$500.00 – 600.00.

Kist Beverages,
Orange Kist
and Other Kist
Beverages,
24" x 8", 1960s,
$150.00 – 200.00.

BEVERAGE

Kist,
39" x 9", 1950s,
$250.00 – 300.00.

Kist
Beverages,
12" dia., 1960s,
$200.00 – 250.00.

Kentucky Tavern,
12", 1950s,
$125.00.

Legra, 25" x 10", 1950, $250.00.

Ma's Old Fashion Root Beer, 26½" x 7", 1944, $175.00 – 225.00.

Mason's Root Beer, painted stamped metal, 25½" x 8", late 1940s, $300.00 – 350.00.

Mason's Root Beer, 25½" x 9½", 1950s – 1960s, $200.00 – 250.00.

Mason's Root
Beer, 12" dia.,
1960s, $150.00.

Mason's
Root Beer,
25½" x 8½",
1950s,
$200.00 – 250.00.

Mason's
Root Beer,
25" x 8", 1950,
$450.00 – 550.00.

Mello Yello,
14" x 4½", 1980s,
$25.00 – 50.00.

Mission Orange,
tin, 15½" x 5½",
1960s,
$100.00 – 150.00.

Mission Orange,
Mission of
California, tin,
17" x 5", 1960s,
$100.00 – 125.00.

Moran's, 16" x 5",
1950s – 1960s,
$125.00.

Mountain Dew,
18" dia., 1980s,
$150.00 – 200.00.

Moxie, 12" dia.,
1950s – 1960s,
$150.00 – 200.00.

Moxie, 12" dia.,
1950s – 1960s,
$150.00 – 200.00.

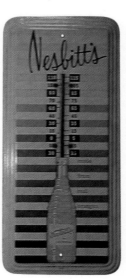

Moxie, 13" x 6",
1950s – 1960s,
$125.00.

Nesbitt's,
27" x 7", 1950s,
$150.00.

Nesbitt's Orange,
16" x 5",
Canadian,
$125.00 – 150.00.

Nesbitt's, tin,
17" x 7½",
1950s, $200.00.

BEVERAGE

Nesbitt's,
27" x 7½",
1960s, $250.00.

Nesbitt's,
27" x 7¼", 1958,
$250.00 – 300.00.

Nesbitt's Orange,
plastic,
22" x 8", 1980s,
hard to find,
$150.00 – 175.00.

NuGrape Soda,
15½" x 7", 1950s,
$200.00 – 250.00.

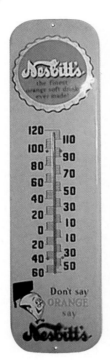

Nugrape, tin,
16" x 5½",
1960s – 1970s,
$75.00 – 100.00.

Nugrape Soda,
diecut,
17" x 5", 1950s,
$200.00 – 250.00.

Nugrape Soda,
12" dia., 1950s,
$225.00.

BEVERAGE

Nugrape Soda,
green, diecut,
17" x 5", 1950s,
$200.00 – 250.00.

Nugrape Soda,
17" x 6", 1950s,
$150.00.

Old Crown,
12" dia., 1990s,
$50.00.

Old Stagg Straight Bourbon, diecut cardboard, 6" x 2", 1970s, $15.00 – 25.00.

Orange Crush, tin, 16" x 6", 1950s, $125.00.

Orange Crush dark green, tin, 16" x 6", 1950s, $125.00.

Orange Crush, 16" x 6½", 1970s, Canadian, $125.00 – 175.00.

Orange Crush,
15" x 6", 1950s,
$300.00.

Orange Crush,
17" x 5", 1960s,
Canadian,
$125.00.

Orange Crush,
diecut,
29" x 7", 1950s,
$300.00 – 325.00.

Orange Crush,
tin, 15" x 6",
1950s,
$350.00 – 400.00.

Orange Crush,
9½" x 3½",
1950s,
$150.00 – 200.00.

Orange Crush,
12" dia., 1960s,
$200.00.

Orange Crush,
12" dia., 1958,
$300.00 – 350.00.

Ortlieb's Premi-
um Lager Beer,
10" dia., 1950s,
$150.00 – 200.00.

O-So Grape,
14" x 4", 1970s,
$75.00.

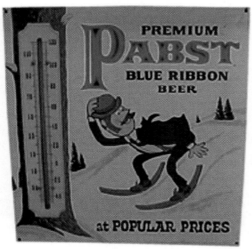

Pabst Blue
Ribbon Beer,
15" x 14", 1960s,
$75.00 – 100.00.

Pabst Blue
Ribbon Beer,
20" x 9", 1970s,
$75.00 – 100.00.

Pabst Blue
Ribbon Beers,
18" x 10", 1960s,
$85.00 – 100.00.

Original Pabst
Blue Ribbon
Beer, 1960s,
$85.00 – 100.00.

Pabst Blue
Ribbon Beer,
20" x 9", 1970s,
$75.00 – 100.00.

Patt's Birch Beer,
9" dia., 1990s,
$50.00 – 75.00.

Pearl, 12" dia.,
1960s – 1970s,
$150.00.

Have a Pepsi,
16" x 6", 1950s,
$125.00 – 150.00.

Say **Pepsi** Please, tin, 27" x 7", 1960s, $75.00 – 100.00.

Pepsi-Cola, The Light Refreshment, raised cap on top, 27" x 7", 1950s, $150.00 – 175.00.

Pepsi, Say "Pepsi, Please," self-framed, 6" glass front, 9" x 9", 1965, $100.00 – 150.00.

BEVERAGE

Pepsi, 26" x 8", 1980s, $75.00.

Pepsi-Cola, 26" x 8", 1980s, $50.00 – 75.00.

Bigger Pepsi-Cola Better, 15" x 6", 1942, $400.00 – 500.00.

Pepsi Light, 24" x 8", 1980s – 1990s, $100.00.

Pepsi, 18" dia.,
1980s, $150.00.

Have a Pepsi,
Pepsi-Cola, cap at
bottom, 27" x 7",
1950s, $175.00.

PepUp,
Big Boy
Beverages, Inc.,
12" dia.,
1930s – 1940s,
$350.00.

Hiram Walker's
Private Cellar,
12" dia., 1960s,
$75.00.

Quench, two sizes, 14" x 6" and 25" x 10", $200.00 – 250.00.

Quiky, two different thermometers, 1970s, $125.00 each.

Red Rock Cola, 16" x 4½", 1970s, $125.00 – 150.00.

Rock Spring Water & Beverages, 12" dia., $250.00.

Rolling Rock
Beer, 29" x 7½",
1990s,
$25.00 – 35.00.

Royal Crown
Cola, 14" x 6",
1950s, $150.00.

Royal Crown
Cola, tin,
14" x 6", 1950s,
$150.00.

Royal Crown
Cola, tin,
14" x 6", 1960s,
$150.00.

RC, Royal
Crown Cola,
13½" x 5½",
1960s,
$75.00 – 100.00.

Royal
Crown Cola,
white arrow, tin,
25" x 9", 1950s,
$150.00.

Royal
Crown Cola ,
yellow arrow,
25" x 10", 1960s,
$100.00 – 125.00.

Royal Crown Cola, RC Cola, tin, 13" x 6", 1960s, $75.00 – 100.00.

RC, 13½" x 5½", 1970s, $75.00.

BEVERAGE

RC,
Royal Crown
Cola, 12" dia.,
1950s,
$250.00 – 300.00.

Rummy
Grapefruit Drink,
tin, 38" x 8",
$175.00 – 200.00.

Schweppes,
12" dia.,
1970s – 1980s,
$100.00 – 125.00.

Schweppes,
12" dia., 1980s,
$100.00 – 125.00.

Seagram's, painted stamped metal, self-framed, 1970s, $50.00 – 75.00.

Seagram's Cooler, 26" x 10½", 1980s, $75.00 – 100.00.

7up, 12" dia., 1970s, $150.00 – 175.00.

7up,
20" x 9", 1960s,
$125.00 – 150.00.

7up, 19" x 5½",
1970s,
$100.00 – 125.00.

7up, aluminum,
Canadian,
17" x 5½",
$125.00.

7up, scale style,
12" dia., 1960s,
$400.00 – 500.00.

7up,
12" dia., 1970s,
$100.00 – 125.00.

7up, red square,
12" dia., 1970s,
$100.00.

7up, The Uncola,
sunburst,
12" dia., 1980s,
$100.00.

7up, "Ca Ravigote,"
Canadian,
porcelain,
15" x 6", 1960s,
$75.00 – 100.00.

Sprite,
12" dia., 1960s,
$225.00 – 250.00.

Squirt, tin,
14" x 6", 1960s,
$200.00.

Squirt,
13½" x 6", 1960s,
$100.00 – 125.00.

Squirt, 27" x 8",
1980, $175.00.

Squirt, 13" x 6",
1970s, $125.00.

Little Squirt, 9",
1960s, $250.00.

Squirt, 13" x 6", 1970s, $125.00.

Suncrest, bottle, tin, 16" x 4", 1960s, $200.00.

Suncrest Beverages, tin, 16" x 6", 1960s, $150.00.

Suncrest, bottle, tin, 17" x 5", 1950s, $225.00.

Suncrest,
12" dia., 1950s,
$220.00 – 225.00.

Suncrest,
12" dia., 1950s,
$225.00 – 250.00.

Sundrop, 12"
dia., 1960s,
$125.00.

Golden Cola,
Sundrop,
26½" x 7½",
1970s,
$150.00 – 175.00.

Sugar Free,
Sundrop,
27" x 7",
$300.00 – 400.00.

Sunkist, cans,
10" x 13", 1980s,
$75.00.

Tab, plastic,
17" x 6¾",
$35.00 – 40.00.

Tab, 12" dia., 1970s, $125.00.

Teem, tin, 28" x 12", 1970s, $100.00 – 125.00.

Pick Up Tom
Collins Jr.,
tin, 25" x 10",
1960s – 1970s,
$200.00 – 225.00.

3V Cola,
12" dia., 1960s,
$150.00 – 200.00.

Triple AAA, 12"
dia., $125.00.

Triple XXX,
27" x 7", 1950s,
$300.00 – 325.00.

TruAde,
14" x 5¾", 1957,
$200.00 – 225.00.

Usher's Scotch
Whiskey,
diecut tin,
30" x 7", 1970s,
$100.00 – 125.00.

Vess Cola,
16" x 4½",
1940s war years,
$300.00 – 350.00.

Vess,
12" dia., 1960s,
$250.00 – 300.00.

BEVERAGE

Hiram Walker's Vodka, 12" dia., 1960s, $100.00 –125.00.

Whistle, 1950s, $400.00 – 450.00.

Whistle, 12" dia., 1930, $750.00 – 800.00.

Wishing Well Orange, painted stamped metal, 19" x 6", 1960s, $300.00 – 350.00.

Yellowstone Whiskey, 14½" x 5½", 1950s, $100.00 – 150.00.

Yellowstone, The No-bite Bourbon, 7" dia., 1980s, $30.00 – 40.00.

FOOD

A-1 Steak Sauce, wood with paper label, 17" x 4½", $25.00 – 35.00.

All-Jersey Milk, cardboard, 7" x 3", $20.00 – 30.00.

Borden Ice Cream, 12" dia., 1950s, $350.00 – 400.00.

Bunny Bread, 12" dia., 1957, $500.00.

Buttercrust Bread, 12" dia., $200.00.

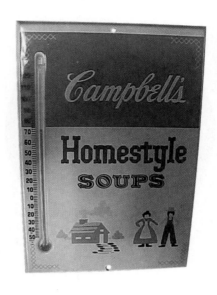

Campbell's Homestyle Soups, originally obtained by sending in a coupon, 9" x 6", 1980s, $65.00 – 85.00.

Jumbo Bread, **Centralia Baking Co.**, Centralia, Ill., 12" dia., $300.00 – 350.00.

Chiquita, Banana Storage Temperature, plastic, 1980s, $50.00 – 75.00.

Clark Bar, wood, 19" x 6", 1930s, $350.00 – 400.00.

40 Fathom Seafood House, metal frame with glass front, 7" x 5", 1950s, $50.00 – 60.00.

Gold Medal Flour, Washburn Crosby, wood with paper label, 18½" x 4½", 1980s, $30.00 – 35.00.

Heide Candies, painted stamped metal, 24" x 8", 1980s, $150.00 – 200.00.

Holland Ice Cream, 12" dia., 1960s, $200.00.

Kern's, Bread, Rolls, Cakes, Cookies, 16" x 6", $125.00.

El Kluener, painted stamped metal, 23" x 8", 1993, $75.00 – 100.00.

Kroger, 12" dia., mid 1960s, $150.00 – 200.00.

FOOD

McDonald's,
wood,
18" x 5½", 1978,
$125.00 – 150.00.

Nusoy Bread,
mirror,
10½" x 14½",
$65.00.

FOOD

Quaker Masa
Harina, diecut
plastic, Mexican,
12" x 8", 1970s,
$65.00 – 85.00.

Quality Checked,
Pure Milk Co.,
6" x 3", 1960s,
$100.00.

Stoutenburg
Dairy,
thermometer
and calendar,
7" x 3", $35.00.

FOOD

Sunbeam Bread,
12" dia., 1950s,
$700.00 – 750.00.

Tender Flake
Flour, 12" dia.,
1960s, $150.00.

Tom's
Toasted Peanuts,
15½" x 6", 1970s,
$40.00 – 50.00.

Pain
Weston Bread,
12" dia., 1960s,
$200.00 – 225.00.

FUNERAL & AMBULANCE

Ambulance
Service, Dial
21193, tin,
13" x 7", 1970s,
$35.00 – 40.00.

E.A. Billman,
Private
Ambulance,
wood, 46" x 8",
$150.00.

Phone C-4351,
Ambulance
Service, **Callahan
Funeral Home**,
cardboard with
calendar,
5" dia., 1942,
$50.00 – 75.00.

**Condo & Sons
Funeral Home**,
metal with glass
front, silhouette,
5" x 4", 1950s,
$35.00 – 50.00.

Crumley Funeral Home, metal frame with glass front, silhouette, 5" x 4", 1950s, $45.00 – 65.00.

A.O. Gillis & Sons Ambulance Service, C-4345, 12" dia., 1960s, $50.00 – 75.00.

Johnson Bros. Funeral Directors, 38" x 8", $225.00.

Reese Funeral Home, 13" x 4", 1950s, $50.00.

Miller and Sons, Brazil, Ind., cardboard, 5" dia., 1950s, $15.00 – 20.00.

Dependable Ambulance and Funeral Service, Clay City, Ind., 13" x 4", 1950s, $45.00.

Andrew Schum and Sons, Phone 167, Dale, Indiana, plastic, 7" dia., 1950s, $35.00.

Ward Funeral Home, 13" x 4", 1950s, $35.00.

Wood Funeral Home, wood, 15" x 4", 1950s, $65.00 – 85.00.

Zieren Funeral Home, Paris Ill., 9" x 4", 1940s, $35.00.

EALTHCARE

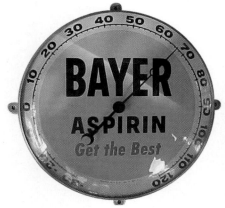

Bayer Aspirin,
12" dia., 1960s,
$300.00 – 350.00.

Calotab's, wood,
15" x 4", 1950s,
$100.00.

Doan's Kidney Pills, wood, 21" x 5", 1930s, $300.00.

Dr. N.L. Bastin, Optometrist, tin, 14" x 5", $75.00.

Dr. Victor P. George, diecut cardboard with calendar, 9½" x 5", 1952, $75.00 – 100.00.

Ex-Lax, The Safe Chocolated Laxative, porcelain on stamped metal, 26" x 8", late 1940s, $350.00 – 450.00.

Ex-Lax, porcelain on stamped metal with horizontal bulb, 36" x 8", $350.00 – 450.00.

Ex-Lax, The Chocolated Laxative, painted metal, 1960s, $100.00 – 150.00.

Ex-Lax for Constipation, porcelain and stamped metal, late 1930s, $400.00 – 500.00.

Frederick Kull, Optometrist & Optician, 21" x 6", $150.00.

Edward Lummis,
Optometrist,
wood, 14½" x 4",
1930s, $150.00.

McKesson's
Aspirin, porce-
lain, 26" x 7",
1930s – 1940s,
$350.00.

NR, procelain, 27" x 7", 1930s, $350.00 – 400.00.

NR, Nature's Remedy, cardboard, 5" x 3", 1950s, $15.00 – 20.00.

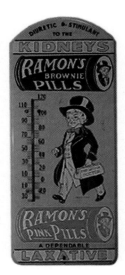

Kidney's Ramon's Brownie Pills, Ramon's Pink Pills, Laxative, tin, 21½" x 9", 1930s, $350.00 – 400.00.

Rexall Drugs, glass test tube, 15" x 2", $850.00 – 1,000.00.

Tums, tin,
9" x 4", 1950s,
$100.00 – 150.00.

Goff's Drug
Store, cardboard
with calendar,
8½" x 3½", 1935,
$35.00 – 50.00.

Vicks, 12" x 4",
1950s, $250.00.

INDUSTRY

B. & W. Coal
Company,
Feed – Lime
Stone Fertilizer
Trucking, Vine
Grove, Ky.,
12" x 3",
late 1940s,
$50.00 – 75.00.

Big Oak Coal Co.,
picture,
9" x 4", 1957,
$35.00 – 45.00.

Briggs and Stratton, glass front, 18½" dia., 1970s, $150.00 – 200.00.

Deep Vein Coal Co., wood, 6½" x 3", 1950s, $65.00 – 85.00.

Gibson Coal Co. Inc., painted stamped metal, 16" x 5", 1950s, $100.00 – 125.00.

KY Lumber Co.,
27" x 8", 1960s,
$65.00.

Lueken & Pund
Lumber Co.,
Ferdinand, Ind.,
7¾" x 2½",
1960s, $20.00.

Lumbermen's Service, wood, 12½" x 4½", 1930s – 1940s, $50.00 – 60.00.

Sahara Coal, O'Gara Coal Company, celluloid with dial thermometer, 3½" dia., 1950s, $75.00 – 100.00.

Sellersburg Lumber & Supply, 12" x 3", 1950s, $50.00.

Southern Ill., Lumber Co., wood, 10" x 4", 1950s, $75.00 – 100.00.

Tretter Lumber Co., 4½" x 12½", 1930s – 1940s, $50.00 – 60.00.

Wice Lumber Co., Greenville, Ky., wood, 10" x 4", 1940s – 1950s, $75.00.

Russell Wilson Coal Co., Evansville, Ind., 1950s, 13" x 4", $50.00.

Joe Camel, painted diecut metal, 18" x 15", $65.00 – 85.00.

Camels, tin, 13" x 6", 1970s, $70.00 – 75.00.

Camels, tin, 13" x 6", 1970s, $70.00 – 75.00.

Carlton Cigarettes, 28" x 7½", 1991, $45.00.

Cash Value Chewing Tobacco, 9½" dia., 1950s – 1960s, $65.00 – 75.00.

Chesterfield, tin, 11" x 5", 1950s, $65.00 – 75.00.

Chesterfield,
13" x 6", 1970s,
$150.00 – 175.00.

Honey Bee,
Sweet Snuff
Smokeless Treat,
tin, 15½" x 6",
1950s,
$200.00.

Kool, Filter Kings
Mild Menthol
Cigarette, tin,
12" x 3½", 1960s,
$50.00 – 75.00.

L & M Cigarettes,
tin, 13" x 6", 1960s,
$65.00 – 85.00.

L & M,
11" x 5", 1950s,
$50.00 – 75.00.

**La Fendrich
Cigar,** Always a
Cool Smoke,
25" x 10",
$450.00.

**Mail Pouch
Tobacco,** tin,
38½" x 8", 1960s,
$75.00 – 100.00.

**Mail Pouch
Tobacco,** porce-
lain, 38" x 7½",
1930s, $200.00.

Marvels Ciga-
rettes, tin,
12" x 4", 1950s,
$150.00.

Marvels, self-
framing print on
metal, 12" x 3¾",
1940s – 1950s,
$200.00 – 250.00.

Oasis Filtered
Cigarettes,
Menthol,
13" x 5½", 1970s,
$125.00 – 150.00.

Marlboro, Philip Morris, tin, 13" x 6", 1960s, $75.00 – 100.00.

Royal Danish Snuff, Smokeless Tobacco Product, 12" dia., 1970s – 1980s, $125.00.

Salem, tin,
10", 1960s,
$50.00 – 60.00.

Union Workman
Chewing Tobacco,
12" dia., 1960s,
$200.00 – 225.00.

Vantage, tin tri-
angle, 9½",
1960s, $75.00.

Winston, Pack or
Box, tin, 9" dia.,
1960s, $75.00.

Winston, 9" dia.,
1960s, $75.00.

Winston, tin,
13" x 6", 1980s,
$60.00.

Winston,
painted blue,
13½" x 6", 1980s,
$65.00 – 75.00.

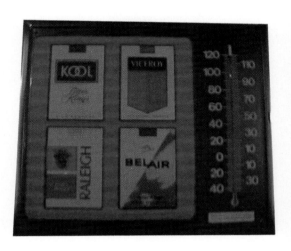

Various
Cigarettes,
Kool, Viceroy,
Raleigh, Belair,
19" x 16½",
$75.00 – 85.00.

ISCELLANEOUS

Anchor, souvenir, 7" x 3½", 1960s, $10.00.

Anderson Windows and Doors, 12" dia., 1980s – 1990s, $75.00.

B & B Heating Co., metal with glass front silhouette, 5" x 4", $35.00 – 50.00.

Bank of Caneyville, 13" x 5", 1960s, $35.00.

Bank of Clarkson, Clarkson, Kentucky, 14" x 4", 1960s, $35.00.

Biltrite Shoes & Soles, 13" x 6", 1950s, $125.00 – 150.00.

Gordon's Potato Chips, leather with a small truck at top, 18" x 5", $50.00.

Bonderia's T.V. Sales and Service, spaniel, 5" x 4", 1950s, $20.00. – 25.00.

Boston Museum of Science, keychain thermometer, 1990s, $3.00 – 5.00.

Boy Scouts of America, keychain thermometer, 1990s, $3.00 – 5.00.

Carter White Lead Paint, embossed porcelain, 27" x 7", $400.00.

MISCELLANEOUS

CEC's Electric, light switch cover, plastic, 5" x 3", 1950s, $10.00 – 15.00.

We Have Filtered Soft Water, Hey Culligan, Man, 12" x 12", 1960s, $100.00 – 125.00.

Curlee Clothes porcelain, 27" x 7", $400.00.

Curtis Windows, Indiana Wholesalers, Inc., 17" x 4", 1960s, $50.00.

Cub Scouts, 16" x 5", 1950s, $75.00 – 100.00.

Desco, 12" dia., 1950s, $125.00 – 150.00.

MISCELLANEOUS

Fydo, Just a Dog,
13" x 3", 1960s,
$10.00.

Droegkamp
Furnaces, scale
type celluloid,
3½" dia.,
$100.00 – 125.00.

Dr. Wells, The Cooler Doctor, made by NuGrape, 15" x 6", $75.00 – 100.00.

Dupont Racing, Jeff Gordon #24, paint on stamped metal, 27" x 8", 1990s, $35.00 – 50.00.

Elliott Equipment Co., Inc., scale type, 8" x 6½", 1980s, $25.00 – 35.00.

Elvis, Some Like It Cool, painted stamped metal, 39" x 8", 1990s, $75.00 – 100.00.

Field's Oil Heat Service, Shell, wood, 8" x 2", $65.00 – 85.00.

Flox Aid, 10" dia., $75.00.

Framed baby, mirror, 14" x 9", 1950s, $60.00.

Framed Native American, beautiful example of thermometers used in the 1940s and 1950s, wood frame with cardboard backing and glass front, all different kinds of pictures were used, 12" x 9", 1940s – 1950s, $50.00 – 75.00.

Framed rendering, 8½" x 2", 1950s, $50.00.

Gates Electric Co., plastic, 7" x 2", 1950s, $50.00 – 65.00.

Gehl fertilizer, 12" dia., 1950s, $75.00 – 100.00.

General Machine and Welding Co., Inc., Cannelton, Ind., wood, 15" x 4", 1940s, $150.00.

Gold Bond Paints, National Gypsum Company, 12" dia., $75.00 – 100.00.

Oven thermometer, **Good Housekeeping**, porcelain, 5½" x 3", 1950s, $45.00 – 65.00.

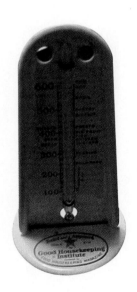

Gray Seal Paint,
12" dia., 1960s,
$100.00.

Guitar, 8",
1950s – 1960s,
$25.00.

Hankins, metal with glass front, silhouette, 5" x 4", 1950s, $35.00 – 50.00.

CSC, Hi-D Ammonium Nitrate, 12" dia., 1950s, $225.00 – 250.00.

Hotel, Princeton, Ky., glass front with standard oil map at bottom, 37" x 12", 1920s, $200.00 – 250.00.

Princeton, Ky., Hotel, enlargement.

Hotel Jefferson,
23" x 6",
1940s – 1950s,
$150.00.

Houk Insurance
Agency, 13" x 4",
1960s – 1970s,
$35.00.

House of Flowers, Madison, Ind., plastic, 7" dia., 1950, $75.00 – 100.00.

Housh Industrial Supplies, tin, 9" x 4", 1950s, $50.00.

Fred Husemann
Bottling Works,
diecut cardboard,
9" x 6½", 1950s,
$75.00 – 85.00.

IFC Friendly
Financing,
12" dia., 1960s,
$100.00.

IPC, Goshen, Ind., metal back with oval test tube, 13" x 5", 1950s – 1960s, $125.00.

J.T. Richardson, Inc., painted stamped metal, 24" x 8", 1980s, $65.00 – 85.00.

Indianapolis Glove Company, 12" dia., 1960s, $150.00 – 175.00.

Kasco Dog Ration, 12" dia., 1960s, $200.00.

Shapleigh's **Keen Kutter**, 12" dia., 1950s, $400.00 – 450.00. Watch for reproductions. Temperature for original goes to 120°. Temperature for reproduction goes to 130°.

Ken-L-Ration, 12" dia., 1950s, $400.00 – 425.00.

Ken-L-Ration, stamped metal, 26½" x 7¼", 1960s, $200.00 – 250.00.

Brass Key, Mississippi Gulf Coast, 7¾" x 3", $25.00.

Brass Key, Mississippi Gulf Coast, enlargement.

Raymond T. Kuester store, Fort Branch, Ind., 13" x 4", 1960s, $35.00.

Krona, 9" glass front, 14" x 11", $300.00 – 350.00.

Larimore Service Station, curved glass with metal fasteners, silhouette, 5" x 4", 1940s, $60.00 – 75.00.

Lawrence Co-operative Creamery Valley Lea Butter, curved glass, silhouette, 4" dia., 1940s, $50.00 – 65.00.

Lilly, plastic, 7" x 2", 1990s, $10.00 – 15.00.

MISCELLANEOUS

Lord Dalton Underwear, 6" dia., 1930s – 1940s, $250.00 – 300.00.

Maple City Truck Line, metal with glass front, silhouette, 10" x 8", 1950s, $85.00 – 100.00.

Merritt Manning Service, light switch cover, plastic, 6" x 3", 1950s, $10.00 – 15.00.

Masonic, plaster, glass front, 5¼" x 4", 1940s, $50.00 – 75.00.

Maxwell Concrete, Tile, Sewer Manholes, tin, 24" x 8", $50.00 – 75.00.

Miller-Johnson Company, 16" x 6", 1940s, $75.00.

Monarch Paint,
porcelain,
38½" x 8",
$225.00.

Motorola,
America's
Finest Radio,
39" x 8", 1960s,
$250.00 – 300.00.

Mystic Weather
Forecaster,
5½" x 4½",
$60.00.

Richard Petty
#43, Nascar,
9" x 6", 1992,
$35.00 – 50.00.

Nationwide
Insurance,
12" dia., 1950s,
$125.00 – 150.00.

MISCELLANEOUS

Oakes Manufacturing Co., Inc., porcelain, 6¼" x 1⅜", 1920s, $50.00 – 75.00.

Omark Oregon Saw Chain and Accessories, 12" dia., 1960s, $75.00 – 100.00.

O's Gold, feeds,
12" dia., 1960s,
$125.00.

OshKosh B'gosh,
Work Wear,
25½" x 9¾",
1950s,
$400.00 – 450.00.

Overhead Door
Co., Inc.,
painted metal,
16" x 5", 1950s,
$85.00 – 100.00.

MISCELLANEOUS

Paducah Burley
Floor, wood,
12" x 3", 1940s,
$100.00.

Penn Reels,
painted stamped
metal, 15½" x 6",
$150.00 – 200.00.

The Perfection
Mfg. Co., Rock-A-
Bye, porcelain,
6" x 2¾",
$175.00 – 200.00.

Peerless
PerfecTemp
Heating & Air
Conditioning,
cardboard,
9" x 3", 1960,
$25.00 – 35.00.

Peters Weather-
bird Shoes,
porcelain on
stamped metal,
26" x 7", 1920s,
$450.00 – 500.00.

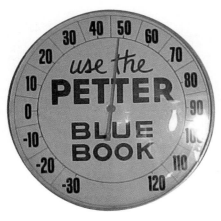

Use the Petter
Blue Book,
12" dia., 1990s,
$75.00.

Use the Petter
Blue Book,
12" dia., 1960s,
$100.00.

Quality Inc.,
Farm and Fleet,
12" dia., 1970s,
$75.00 – 100.00.

Red Goose Shoes, plastic goose with 10" glass front, 25" x 13", $250.00 – 300.00.

Red Goose School Shoes, porcelain on stamped metal, 27½" x 7", 1920s, $350.00 – 400.00.

MISCELLANEOUS

Rich-Law Service Co., FS, painted plastic, 7" x 2½", 1950s, $100.00 – 125.00.

Support Reelsville Baseball Teams, Little League and Pee Wee Teams, painted stamped metal, 16" x 4½", 1950s, $100.00 – 125.00. These were sold by Kidson Fundraiser for ball clubs.

Ruth Beauty Shop, metal frame with silhouette border, 5" x 4", 1950s, $25.00 – 35.00.

Schauerte Tailors
Belleville, Ill.,
wood, 15" x 4",
1930s,
$75.00 – 100.00.

Scott Towels,
print on wood,
17" x 8½", 1981,
$45.00 – 65.00.

Boy Scout on
Farmer Bank,
9½" x 6¾",
early 1900,
$75.00 – 100.00.

Seat Covers, tin,
26" x 7", 1950s,
$150.00.

Sebree Deposit
Bank, 1890 –
1990, Sebree,
Kentucky, tin,
10" x 6", 1990s,
$35.00.

Shannon Com-
mission Co., tin,
6" x 2", 1950s,
$25.00.

Little Shovel,
7" x 2", $35.00.

**Simplified Refrig-
eration**, refrigera-
tor thermometer,
tin self hanger,
3½" x 3", 1940s,
$40.00 – 50.00.

Snap-On Tools,
tin, 14" x 4",
1970s, $40.00.

Harry Skinner & Sons, Bakelite scale type, 7" x 6½", 1940s, $50.00 – 75.00.

Sterling Salt, 12" dia., 1960s, $125.00.

Stihl, glass front, 12" dia., 1970s – 1980s, $100.00.

Stihl, plastic face, 12", 1980s, $30.00 – 40.00.

Straus Credit Jewelers, metal frame with glass front, silhouette, 5" x 4", 1950s, $35.00 – 50.00.

Sylvania Radios, 12" dia., 1959, $550.00 – 650.00.

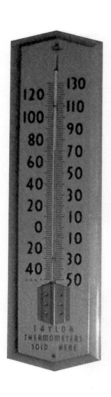

Tayor Thermometers, painted wood, 28½" x 7½", 1940s, $250.00 – 300.00 rare.

The Tway Co., Inc., Cable Co., 9" x 4", $35.00 – 50.00.

MISCELLANEOUS

U-Haul Rentals,
scale style with
glass front,
13½" dia.,
$500.00 – 550.00.

Union Label
Shirts, 27" x 4½",
$150.00.

University Shoe Renewing Shop, metal with glass front, 7" x 5", 1950s, $35.00 – 50.00.

U.S.S. American Fence and Posts, porcelain, stamped metal, 19" x 6", 1930s, $100.00 – 125.00.

Vigo Ice and Cold Storage Co., tin, 16" x 5", 1950s, $65.00 – 75.00.

Weather-Bird Shoes, Peters Shoe Co., 38" x 8", $250.00 – 300.00.

West KY Rural Electric, 9" x 3", 1960s, $20.00.

Wholesale Florist, Flowers and Supplies, porcelain, 13" x 4", $50.00.

Winchester AA
Clay Target
Ammunition,
27" x 8", 1970s,
$150.00 – 200.00.

Winchester,
9½" x 2½",
1990s,
$20.00 – 25.00.

Winchester,
27" x 8", 1990s,
$35.00 – 45.00.

The Wolf
Machine Co.
Cloth Cutters,
9" x 4", 1950s,
$35.00.

Zimmerman
Brothers, card-
board with match
holder at bottom,
14½" x 10", 1914,
$75.00 – 100.00.

COLLECTOR BOOKS
Informing Today's Collector

GLASSWARE & POTTERY

4929	American Art Pottery, 1880 – 1950, Sigafoose	$24.95
5358	Coll. Ency. of Depression Glass, 14th Ed., Florence	$19.95
5040	Collector's Encyclopedia of Fiesta, 8th Ed., Huxford	$19.95
1358	Collector's Encyclopedia of McCoy Pottery, Huxford	$19.95
5255	Collector's Guide to Camark Pottery, Gifford	$19.95
2339	Collector's Guide to Shawnee Pottery, Vanderbilt	$19.95
5528	Early American Pattern Glass, Metz	$17.95
5617	Ency. of Pressed Glass, 2nd Ed., Edwards/Carwile	$29.95
5257	Fenton Art Glass Patterns, 1939 – 1980, Whitmyer	$29.95
5261	Fostoria Tableware, 1924 – 1943, Long/Seate	$24.95
5279	Glass Toothpick Holders, Bredehoft/Sanford	$24.95

OTHER COLLECTIBLES

2269	Antique Brass & Copper Collectibles, Gaston	$16.95
1880	Antique Iron, McNerney	$9.95
3872	Antique Tins, Dodge	$24.95
1128	Bottle Pricing Guide, 3rd Ed., Cleveland	$7.95
3718	Collectible Aluminum, Grist	$16.95
4852	Collectible Compact Disc Price Guide 2, Cooper	$17.95
4705	Collector's Guide to Antique Radios, 4th Ed., Bunis	$18.95
3880	Collector's Guide to Cigarette Lighters, Flanagan	$17.95
3881	Collector's Guide to Novelty Radios, Bunis/Breed	$18.95
4652	Collector's Gde to Transistor Radios, 2nd Ed., Bunis	$16.95
1629	Doorstops, Identification & Values, Bertoia	$9.95
5683	Fishing Lure Collectibles, 2nd Ed.Murphy/Edmisten	$29.95
5259	Flea Market Trader, 12th Ed., Huxford	$9.95
3819	General Store Collectibles, Wilson	$24.95
2216	Kitchen Antiques, 1790–1940, McNerney	$14.95
2026	Railroad Collectibles, 4th Ed., Baker	$14.95
1632	Salt & Pepper Shakers, Guarnaccia	$9.95
5091	Salt & Pepper Shakers II, Guarnaccia	$18.95
2220	Salt & Pepper Shakers III, Guarnaccia	$14.95
3443	Salt & Pepper Shakers IV, Guarnaccia	$18.95
5007	Silverplated Flatware, Revised 4th Edition, Hagan	$18.95
1922	Standard Old Bottle Price Guide, Sellari	$14.95
3892	Toy & Miniature Sewing Machines, Thomas	$24.95
5144	Value Gde to Advertising Memorabilia, Summers	$19.95
3977	Value Guide to Gas Station Memorabilia, Summers	$24.95
4877	Vintage Bar Ware, Visakay	$24.95
5281	Wanted to Buy, 7th Edition	$9.95

TOYS, MARBLES & CHRISTMAS COLLECTIBLES

3427	Advertising Character Collectibles, Dotz	$17.95
2333	Antique & Collectible Marbles, 3rd Ed., Grist	$9.95
2338	Collector's Encyclopedia of Disneyana, Longest, Stern	$24.95

4958	Collector's Guide to Battery Toys, Hultzman	$19.95
4566	Collector's Guide to Tootsietoys, 2nd Ed, Richter	$19.95
4945	G-Men and FBI Toys, Whitworth	$18.95
5593	Grist's Big Book of Marbles, 2nd Ed.	$24.95
5267	Matchbox Toys, 3rd Ed., 1947 to 1998, Johnson	$19.95
4871	McDonald's Collectibles, Henriques/DuVall	$19.95
1540	Modern Toys 1930–1980, Baker	$19.95
2028	Toys, Antique & Collectible, Longest	$14.95

DOLLS, FIGURES & TEDDY BEARS

2079	Barbie Doll Fashion, Volume I, Eames	$24.95
3957	Barbie Exclusives, Rana	$18.95
4557	Barbie, The First 30 Years, Deutsch	$24.95
3810	Chatty Cathy Dolls, Lewis	$15.95
4559	Collectible Action Figures, 2nd Ed., Manos	$17.95
4863	Collector's Encyclopedia of Vogue Dolls, Stover/Izen	$29.95
4861	Collector's Guide to Tammy, Sabulis/Weglewski	$18.95
5599	Dolls of the 1960s and 1970s, Sabulis	$24.95
5598	Doll Values, Antique to Modern, 4th Ed., Moyer	$12.95
1799	Effanbee Dolls, Smith	$19.95
5610	Madame Alexander Price Guide #25, Crowsey	$9.95
5612	Modern Collectible Dolls, Volume IV, Moyer	$24.95
5368	Schroeder Collectible Toys, 6th Ed., Huxford	$17.95
5253	Story of Barbie, 2nd Ed., Westenhouser	$24.95
1513	Teddy Bears & Steiff Animals, Mandel	$9.95
1817	Teddy Bears & Steiff Animals, 2nd Series, Mandel	$19.95
1808	Wonder of Barbie, Manos	$9.95
1430	World of Barbie Dolls, Manos	$9.95
4880	World of Raggedy Ann Collectibles, Avery	$24.95

INDIANS, GUNS, KNIVES, TOOLS, PRIMITIVES

1868	Antique Tools, Our American Heritage, McNerney	$9.95
1426	Arrowheads & Projectile Points, Hothem	$7.95
2279	Indian Artifacts of the Midwest, Hothem	$14.95
3885	Indian Artifacts of the Midwest, Book II, Hothem	$16.95
2164	Primitives, Our American Heritage, McNerney	$9.95

PAPER COLLECTIBLES & BOOKS

4710	Collector's Guide to Children's Books, Jones	$18.95
5153	Collector's Guide to Children's Books, Vol. 2, Jones	$19.95
5596	Collector's Guide to Children's Books, Vol. 3, Jones	$19.95
1441	Collector's Guide to Post Cards, Wood	$9.95
2081	Guide to Collecting Cookbooks, Allen	$14.95
5613	Huxford's Old Book Value Guide, 12th Ed.	$19.95
4654	Victorian Trade Cards, Cheadle	$19.95
4733	Whitman Juvenile Books, Brown	$17.95

This is only a partial listing of the books on collectibles that are available from Collector Books. All books are well illustrated and contain current values. Most of our books are available from your local bookseller, antique dealer, or public library. If you are unable to locate certain titles in your area, you may order by mail from COLLECTOR BOOKS, P.O. Box 3009, Paducah, KY 42002-3009. Customers with Visa, MasterCard, or Discover may phone in orders from 7:00–5:00 CST, Monday–Friday, Toll Free 1-800-626-5420; www.collectorbooks.com. Add $3.00 for postage for the first book ordered and 50¢ for each additional book. Include item number, title, and price when ordering. Allow 14 to 21 days for delivery.